Poems of Perception

Poems Written by Brian Geerdts
Cover & Interior Photographs by Brian Geerdts
Layout & Design by Griffin Mill

ISBN: 978-1-957351-69-8

Published by Nico 11 Publishing & Design
Mukwonago, Wisconsin
www.nico11publishing.com

Be well read.

Quantity purchase requests can be emailed to:
mike@nico11publishing.com

Printed in the United States of America

POEMS OF PERCEPTION

Perception is a word with limitless possibilities. How one person views a situation many times is completely different than another's observation. That is the beauty. We all have our own eyes and get to choose what we see with them. The overall interpretation leaves us with our thoughts which form our opinions; ultimately leading to the values in which we lead life. We as humans bear a responsibility to each other. Information that does not tally with our imagination should not be rejected but welcomed as knowledge to our ignorant mind. Happiness and distress come and go like winter turns to summer. Arisen from perception, one must learn tolerance without disrupting the soul. A person cannot bring peace to the world if they can't be at peace with themselves. Things happen for a reason, and I believe that you were destined to read and study these poems. They come from the heart inspired by the world we live in. The commonality preaches to what's left of our integrity. Time is running out for us to do the right thing. The ethical thing.

Table of Contents

chapter one

LIFE

Everyone has a story.
Their trials and tribulations.
Hardships, limitations.
Setbacks and altercations.
Pride, reputations.
Racism and demonstrations.
Goals, justifications.
Dreams and manifestations.
Triumphs, invocations.
Accomplishments and innovations.
Greed, temptations.
Honesty and considerations.
Hard work, determination.
Ethics and accreditation.
Religion, salvation.
Creativity and formulations.
Independence, liberation.
Tragedy and exploitation.
Virtue, interpretations.
Love and communication.
Labels, classifications.
Preparing future generations.
Humanity with no discrimination.

Time and money.

Two things we could use more of.

Dollars so elusive.

The end so conclusive.

Scramble to accomplish everything.

Enjoying the moments that families bring.

Having the means to make your dreams.

Isn't that what we all want in this world.

Endless emotions, wind whirled.

The race for wealth.

Ever so conscious about your health.

Even spending money to increase time by going under the knife.

Time and money are the two most important things in life.

Balancing that is a trick worse than hardship and strife.

An inner struggle of emotion.
Heart causing a commotion.
Brain going in two different directions.
Constantly examining options and past reflections.
Which path is best to take.
What is best for family sake.
Wrestling with decisions to make.
A man's life at stake.
Times good and bad tug at conscience.
How to play out the remainder of existence.
Love conquers all and that's what counts.
Family forever even as tension mounts.
All in this together.
No matter the hardship of any endeavor.

A party with old friends, but strangers remain.
A long-lost friendship you hope to again reclaim.
Fun and laughter are the sounds that fill the room.
Stories of parties and concerts on shrooms.
Somehow, we made it through without a bump or bruise.
The party ended without us knowing it.
The friendship grown stronger without any of us showing it.
Back to our lives with no reunion in sight.
But knowing the chance remains, leaves the future bright.

No answers given.

No hope of getting one.

Survival uncertain.

Waiting.

Waiting for what is to come.

Unsure when it will arrive.

Help!

Clinging to the thought of it.

Engulfing your every desire.

No strength to get through alone.

Mind fading but must stay strong.

Help must come.

An answer has to be given.

The wait must end.

Helplessness.

When you vote, don't decide based on a particular party.
Choose a candidate that will make the country
the most robust and hearty.
Beware of the misinformed and terrible media clouding you.
Use your head and vote for the one your conscience tells you to.
It's our tax dollars that run the government.
Shouldn't the goal of humanity be our testament.
Not just to keep the status quo of this tyranny rule.
Rather run the country for the people and not like a fool.
The responsibility to be ethical and humane is upon us.
Not to just elect another party candidate to whom you distrust.

Life

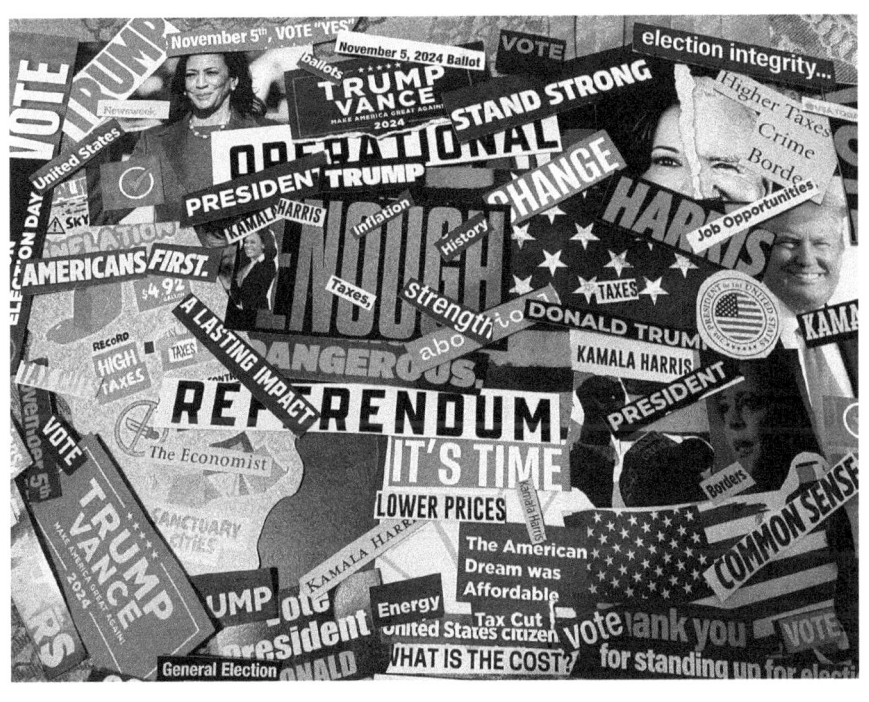

The wheel goes round and round.

No one knows up or down.

What is the secret of life.

Is it kids and a wife.

Sitting in the parking lot binging on ice cream.

Is that living the dream?

Or working your body to death making it a temple.

All while driving yourself mental.

The secret of life is pain and strife.

The wheel still going round and round.

Running steadily along the ground.

Sometimes the road of life will be crappy.

So, concentrate on what makes you happy.

Work hard and enjoy each meal.

Because we only get one chance on this wheel.

Life

Sitting on my couch with a beer.

Enjoying the day off from my career.

Broadcasting sports for a living is what I hold dear.

So, I'm sitting on my couch with a beer.

Glad the TV is coming in clear.

Watching players that come on cards like
Topps, Score, and Fleer.

Some of them I've come to know and revere.

The end of the game is coming near.

And the day is fading fast, I fear.

Time for one more beer.

Back to work tomorrow without shedding a tear.

Back to the career which I hold so dear.

A family of lives intertwined.

Impossible to take the time to unwind.

The burden of responsibility.

Trying to deliver its message with sensibility.

Exhaustion, stress, and hardship combined.

All while keeping composure defined.

Preparing the children to face a harsh future.

Spoken words and posted pictures can't be repaired with a suture.

Be cautious and careful along the way.

But also inspired and challenged every day.

Heal the world is the message to send.

Having the power to change things, your success will depend.

Waiting to Die.

Lying in bed all day watching television.

Stubbornly aware of the decision.

I once was a badass with muscles all over my body.

Trust me when I tell you; I was a hottie.

I could have maintained, but don't know why.

Maybe it was the booze or just being lazy.

I must be honest; my memory is a bit hazy.

I thought I was invincible and could fly.

Nothing could hurt me and believe me I tried.

Prescriptions for mental illness leaves my brain fried.

So, I'm just lying here waiting to die.

Past actions leave me bitter and lonely.

Man, if I could just get a sandwich with liverwurst and bologna.

If I would have put in some effort I could have gotten by.

It's the choices I've made and how I lived my life, so now I'm just waiting to die.

chapter two

LOVE

For your love, I would travel to the moon.
Your beauty makes all heads turn when you walk in the room.
Intelligence of your mind is more attractive than your physique.
Makes me need to step up my game and polish my technique.
Even if the future looks dark and bleak.
Where passion is strained, and patience is weak.
Trust in the love we share to reign supreme.
A life together forever is the ultimate dream.

Love

Our lives intertwined.

Our souls combined.

Hearts together.

Touch soothing, and light as a feather.

Smile that melts the hardships.

Makes me want to gently kiss those lips.

Brightening the outlook on the future.

A love of children excited to nurture.

Two of us can get through anything.

Positivity, laughter, and even when we sing.

River of love flowing through our hearts.

The strength of infinite affection will conquer any issue that starts.

Love

How can you describe the one you love.

Like God sent her just for me from above.

Her smile, laugh, silliness, and charm.

Any guy would be lucky to have her on his arm.

Creative, caring, and common sense.

Her knowledge and leadership shine when situations get tense.

The kind of woman that makes you want to be a better man.

Matching her patience and mental toughness is a task I'm not sure I can.

The kindness in her heart is one to be admired.

Can't resist cuddling even when I'm tired.

The one I would go the distance for.

With her the world I would love to explore.

So how do I describe the beautiful woman I love?

It's a lot more than just the reasons above.

My life has taken me far along earth's land.
Some experiences have been magnificent.
Other days not working out as planned.
Learning and being tough so I don't seem so innocent.
Standing up on my two feet.
Fighting for my place and managing the fear.
Never leaving the job until the work is complete.
Living by my word, honest and sincere.
Finding the love of my life.
A woman who I would go to the moon for.
Love so perfect I made her my wife.
Raising kids, protecting them, trying to give them more.
Seems endless what I have to teach them yet.
Maybe some words of inspiration.
Something that the ones who come after me will never forget.
Always be confident about the decisions you make;
and great achievements require heart and perspiration.

Love

Waking up in your arms is pure heaven.

On a scale, my love for you is an eleven.

Excited that you are my past, present, and future.

An amazing mother dedicated to the boys growing up with
knowledge and nurture.

A perfect woman who deserves to be celebrated.

A beauty so intense keeps everyone captivated.

An intelligence knowing how life can be
improved and innovated.

Never again will a flawless woman such as this ever be recreated.

Love

The eternal love for a child.
An animal being born in the wild.
The dew on a petal in the morning sun.
Clearing your head with a calming run.
Tranquil sounds from a babbling brook.
Feeling free after acing a test you just took.
The gentle touch from the one you love.
Faith reaching out to us from above.
Relaxing with nothing in the world to do.
Fireworks with colors bursting so true.
Happiness on someone's face.
A dancer in all their grace.
Worries melted completely away.
The view of living for today.
Beauty is all over the place.
Realize it can be as infinite as space.

Be grateful for each day.
Time to dream, to improve, to play.
Breathing air gives you a fighting chance.
To touch someone's heart and have that last dance.
Holding your loved ones close or calling a friend on the phone.
Trying something new could be the greatest you've ever known.
Every morning presents a new opportunity.
To be grateful and preach unity.
None of us are better than the other.
At the core we are all a child, a sister, a brother.
So, stand up and believe in what you say.
And be grateful for each and every day.

Love

As you walk through this door.

Feast your eyes like you never have before.

Dreams and fantasies entangled into one.

A visit to confession after all is said and done.

The pleasure is blinding and too much to endure.

Saving a memento just to be sure.

Chemistry that is like fusion in a bottle.

She looks more beautiful than a fashion model.

The eagerness to rush but dying to go slow.

Head spinning with so much excitement it's about to blow.

An experience shared with the love of your life.

It's no secret why you just took her as your wife.

Love

Looking into your eyes.

There is no way to disguise.

My eternal love for you.

Pinch me, I can't believe it's true.

Feeling your soft skin.

Not knowing where to begin.

The overwhelming feeling of attraction.

Sends my head spinning in different directions.

So much beauty in front of my face.

I know I was destined to be in this place.

I love you so much it makes me cry.

Your inspiration makes me think I can fly.

Seeing you smile is the highlight of my day.

Excited for our future, as we make our way.

chapter three

HUMANITY

A friendly nod.

Smiling at someone you don't know.

Lending a hand to a person in need.

A donation to help a child grow.

Caring for another's well-being.

Holding the door for a stranger.

Listening to opposing opinions gives the idea what their seeing.

Leaving labels out of the equation.

Courtesy without judgement.

Business driven by ethics without profit's persuasion.

Being selfless and setting a positive example is smart.

Be righteous and be proud of your actions.

And live with humanity in your heart.

People are the same from every place and street.

They just want to live good and have something to eat.

Yearning for respect and power in their lives.

They want to make a better life for their children to make sure their future thrives.

Just like a tree starts from seed.

We all need to grow and watch out for our needs.

Not be blinded by the ones that consume our existence.

Rather have the tendency to strive with confidence and persistence.

Born into this world.

We are vulnerable to all.

Hoping that love comes to call.

Pressures and decisions take us down our path.

Make the right ones.

Or suffer the aftermath.

Reach for the stars and go for yours.

Indulge your mind in possibilities.

Let your imagination soar.

Break the chains of life.

Starting clean and new.

Free from the old pain and strife.

Do what you love.

Deaf to the ones who doubt.

Climbing the ladder and rising above.

Into your soul you must explore.

Embrace the transformation.

And reach for more.

You can't wish for it; you must put in the work.

Not falling victim to where the distractions lurk.

Give it your all and strive for perfection.

After time you will be proud of your reflection.

Commit yourself offering everything to reach your goal.

Don't be dragged down when hardships take their toll.

Push yourself and chase your dreams.

Once you form the habit of dedication it won't be as bad as it seems.

Inspiration is all around us.
You just must keep your head up and eyes clear.
Something little like a helping hand from a friend.
Staying with an unconscious human till their eyes peer.
Acting as if you don't care is nothing to pretend.
Or words of pride and encouragement from a parent.
Holding the door open for a stranger.
Seeing the soul of someone transparent.
Helping to save a person from danger.
Humanity can be found if you have the courage to be one.
The selflessness and sense to care for an unknown being.
Uplifting children with positive words or actions can be quite fun.
Inspiration is all around us; the trick is seeing.

Lend a hand to another.

Do as much as you would for a brother.

We must extinguish our selfish ways.

Put away the image you like to portray.

Drop the labels and past discrimination.

Stop the greed of business and deforestation.

Help the children living in the street.

Famine is our demise if we don't get enough to eat.

The message must be truly felt by the rich and powerful.

Or this world will fall into chaos and be dreadful.

A new day's blossom of hope can be infectious.

The love and care for a stranger is precious.

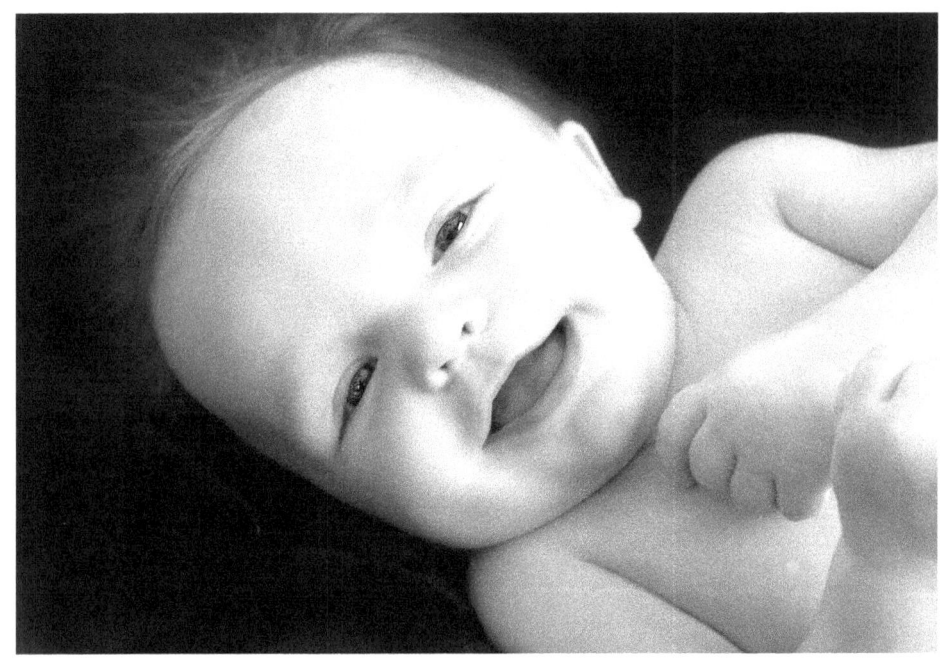

The heart is the first muscle a baby uses in the womb.
It can be wide open or locked up like a tomb.
Controlling the blood that flows.
Reliving the moments where your character shows.
Having the courage to shine and lead the way.
Deciding to care and live for today.
Where you carry your loved ones past and present.
Exercise to make it strong so that your health is pleasant.
Getting knocked down and having the strength to rise back to your feet.
A place where greatness and motivation are not afraid of the heat.
The heart is ability to flood with emotions or be cold as ice.
Even if it breaks, it has the power to heal up nice.
Be careful how you use it.
It can stop at any minute if you abuse it.
So powerful it can be transferred to save another.
A place where confidence and protectiveness lay undercover.
It can turn cold and lifeless while the person still breathes.
When experiencing a loss, every heart greaves.

Anger is a powerful force that can drive a man.

Like an atom bomb causing the most destruction it can.

The warmth and determination arise when trying to prove the world is not right.

Not feeling any pain combined with adrenaline during a fight.

Buried deep inside from a turmoiled place in the past.

Driving rage with no way of telling how long it will last.

Unable to let go and praying that the feeling will pass.

All the while keeping certain aspects of life at a distance.

Striving for perfection and having persistence.

Anger can be an ally if you know how to control it.

Or slowly eating away at your soul, leaving you empty and unfit.

There must be a way a person can let go.

To have inner peace and get on with the show.

The trick is to look and find out how.

To heal, there is no better time to start than now.

Humanity

A place to relax from the stresses of the day.

Where all your cares melt away.

A place that confidence is high.

Where you can dream about your piece of the pie.

A place to belt out like you are an award-winning singer.

Where you imagine yourself in the championship
game hitting a dinger.

A place to formulate your master plans.

Where you make enough money to fill a stadium and its stands.

A place with no judgements whether your too fat or thin.

Where the soothing warmth of the water rains on your skin.

A place when your time is done, you want to turn around and begin.

Thoughts in one's mind.

Sometimes the visions are of negativity or treating someone unkind.

The stress of providing leads to conclusion not so simple to find.

Repetitive songs, phrases, and things to do cloud the brain when all you want to is to unwind.

Getting a chance to look at the sky and dream about what life could be.

Like being a kid when anything was possible and that feeling of living free.

To claim the respect every person deserves.

Far from the hardship everyone endures.

Having peace that life can and will be better.

The prerogative to go and do whatever.

We all can find our subliminal beach.

Just get up each day and manifest your goal to keep it in reach.

Humanity

We are all connected to each.

From border to border.

As far as any eye can reach.

Beyond mountains and seas.

Higher than any brick and mortar.

The one who are enslaved or rejected.

The humans that are mistreated and neglected.

We are all connected.

Hand by hand.

Heart by heart touching every soul.

To every living thing across the land.

Regret and grief will tear a hole in your heart.

Healing comes only if you choose to start.

Time and determination are the keys.

Stay calm and set your mind at ease.

Life will continue even when knocked to your knees.

Some will stare and some may tease.

Listen to other's opinions only if you please.

Do what makes you happy and live your own way.

Eyes on your goals and never stray.

To keep from having more grief and regret someday.

chapter four

NATURE

Clouds go by like smoke from a fire.
Millions stop to look up in a trance to admire.
None knowing one another or what they're worth.
For miles covering the sky engulfing the earth.
Sharing the same experience if only for a moment.
Connected by our genetic makeup and each human component.
Any ill will towards each other, we must make atonement.
Subliminal connection in common given at birth.
Gratitude and positivity are the only way to rejoice with mirth.

The glorious rose.

Whose beauty shines in its distinguished pose.

The intricacies of the stem and petals.

Catching the rain for a drink where it settles.

For deep in the ground are roots growing strong.

Rising each spring healthy and long.

Living and breathing like the rest of us do.

Spreading the symbol of love to hearts through and through.

Admire the glorious rose and don't blink.

Sparking memories as you gaze and think.

Remembering the loved ones, you once knew.

Keeping your heart open and true.

Shells

They come in many different sizes, shapes, and colors.

All unique in their design distinguishes them from all others.

Yet, they are all shells.

Marinated with the salty ocean water smells.

Neither wondering which one is better or worse.

None caring if there is a pearl inside that purse.

All different living in a community of equality.

The beach as their burial ground resting together in harmony.

A bright spring morning so crisp and new.
A start so beautiful, but only admired by a few.
The birds singing their cheerful melody.
The harmonious music ensures their love and fidelity.
Trees shaking off that winter freeze.
Reaching for the warm rays and letting its branches
sway in the breeze.
The grass turning green with colors so deep and true.
The sky, a magnificent blue.
A chance for the earth to be reborn.
Forgetting the cold that leaves it tattered and torn.
Plants breathing new life and starting on their path.
Sleepy animals going down to the river for a quick bath.
Taking in such a sight is like gazing at a priceless piece of art.
The winds each spring mark a fresh start.

Every rock has a story.

Molded and shaped in all its glory.

Ruggedly standing the test of time.

Some no bigger than a dime.

Solid muscle making up its capacity.

Holding strong under pressure with relentless tenacity.

They never fear or have a worry.

Contemplating their next move, but never in a hurry.

Never faltering through any weather.

Bonds are tighter when banded together.

Always steadfast with a crushing grip

Still surviving with a crack or chip.

Every rock has their moments.

Displaying complex crystals and components.

The rain so cold and dreary.

Everyday living makes one feel sick and weary.

But the rain renews the precious land.

Roots grow deeper so the ground is solid where we stand.

Humans planting the seeds to lend a helping hand.

So, the landscape of the earth is breathtakingly grand.

Simply remember, that the rain renews.

No matter what your views.

You can stay in or go out in it if you choose.

Rain equals life; just follow the clues.

For good or for bad.

When it's raining, be glad.

The wind blows.

But no one knows.

Why does the wind come and go?

Why do the weeds grow?

Why does the sun sometimes never show?

Chattering cold from head to toe.

Making the trees wain and woe.

All in tune with the wind's musical flow.

Sometimes straight like an arrow shot from a bow.

Other days are calm and slow.

Take notice to the symphony the wind can bestow.

The tranquil flakes floating to the ground.

Making the leaves so heavy that they dive to their winter resting place in a single bound.

A glimpse of peace watching the snowflakes fall.

A blanket of white covering the houses, streets, cars, and all.

The tingling pain of blue icy feet.

While walking your daily beat.

The bitter cold the snow brings.

Makes one want to hunker down and await the sweet aromas of spring.

Giving plants and soil the nutrients it needs to grow.

Others love the snow and the freshness of a cold wind blow.

Constructing a snowman or on your snowboard feeling the flow.

To snowmobiling to the middle of nowhere just to make an angel because you have the dough.

Laughter echoing from the hills as the sleds speed down.

Not a single child wearing a frown.

The winter wonderland creates beautiful memories for families to share.

A symbol of peace and love to the ones who dare.

It is always running, never getting tired.
If you don't abide by it, you might get fired.
People try to save it whenever they can.
Some like to waste it going into a shop to get a fake tan.
No one has ever beaten it.
Some fall before it because they wouldn't quit.
It's been there since the very beginning.
Must be managed in the interest of winning.
Elusive as a jackrabbit.
Squandering it would be a destructive habit.

The calming rhythm the drops make as they fall to the ground.

Like a symphony arranged by God letting the world
hear the soothing sound.

Filling the rivers and lakes, flooding in as much as they can take.

Sustaining life to the plants and animals leaving a cool drink for all
those in its wake.

Water holds the key to life and how we survive.

It is healing to the soul providing the renewed energy to strive.

As healing as a spa day and as pure as the tase of honey
straight from the hive.

Be grateful when you see rain even though the
darkness can bring pain.

Dwelling on your sadness will bring absolutely nothing to gain.

In all its glory and tranquility, the waterfall stands
in its majestic nobility.

Displaying its power and aggressive ability.

Throwing tons of water per second off a cliff with furious instability.

Yet the grace and beauty of the sight leaves one
with a warm sense of security.

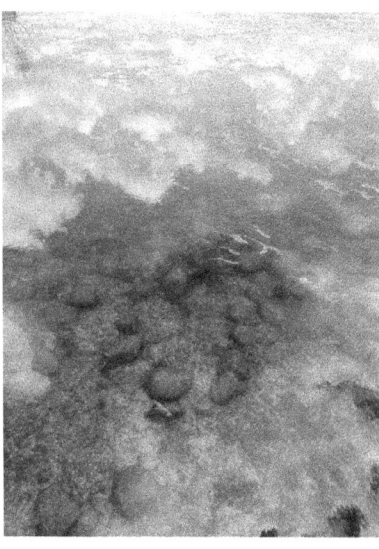

chapter five

GUIDANCE

Guidance

We are all humans.
So, start acting like it.
Color, religion, and language.
We are all humans.
Because we are different.
No need to throw a fit.
Over money, power, and land.
We are all humans.
All existing together.
Available to lend a hand.

Don't label me.

Call me a rebel just because we had a party and dumped some tea.

Or unruly because I choose to fight oppression and try to flee.

I am not a color or a member of a race.

A person is what I am; two eyes, a nose, and lips on my face.

Just a person here in a particular time and place.

Claiming the right to my personal space.

A unique individual is what you see standing here.

It doesn't matter what I believe, where I came from,
or if I am straight or queer.

If you open your heart and get to know me, I may become a peer.

The judging started with your eyes I am beginning to fear.

So let me make this perfectly clear.

I am me and that is all there is to adhere.

Every good thing in life starts with an idea.
The need to accept a person as they are.
Not where they live or the cost of their car.
Releasing the death grip of greed in one's soul.
Disavowing the ego before it gets out of control.
Let love penetrate every part of yourself.
Take hate and anger and place it on the shelf.
Embracing presence in the universe and just be.
Open your eyes to take a glimpse and see.
Brush off the negative and the bad.
Let go of the depression that makes you sad.
Breathe in positivity and an outlook renewed.
It's a beautiful world once it's viewed.

Barriers blocking your path.

Some let them stop you to avoid the wrath.

Naively making the same mistakes time and again.

When will commonsense take over and humanity begin?

Unveiling the curtain shielding our eyes.

Seeing the truth behind the powerful disguise.

All for profit to keep lining their pockets.

Say we're going green while dependent on fossils still on the docket.

Nostradamus could see humanity's writing on the wall.

Knowing when crisis will hit, and empires will fall.

Histories of cultures and countries repeating the same mistakes.

Consuming resources and people to be as rich and powerful as it takes.

We must break the barriers blocking our path.

Prepare yourself and use common sense to do the math.

Angry at the world trends.

And the negativity never ends.

Constantly screwed over by corporations.

Or cops making up false citations.

All for the corruption to continue.

Just pass it on to the consumer on the menu.

The politics of parents in small towns.

Or a CEO making a salary beyond leaps and bounds.

A world designed for the rich to prosper.

And leave what's left of society in the dumpster.

Wealthy bending the law to benefit thy self.

Passing on transgressions to their kids while in deteriorating health.

The world run by old money and corporations.

Not by government organizations.

People who don't obey the law.

Like a dog scratching up the furniture with his paw.

Walking out in front of a moving car without looking.

Only getting a sorry when a business totally botches, you're booking.

Nonexistent customer service.

Doctors misdiagnose and never seem nervous.

Money and power are the priority.

The ones who really care are in the minority.

We humans are to blame for what we've done to each other.

How about a change, respect one another.

When you judge someone, it doesn't define them, it defines you.

The pain and sorrow of the common.

Out there barely able to afford Ramen.

Eyes wide shut by the upper class.

Thinking they help by donating to charity and charging by the glass.

Some get to the top with hard work and determination.

Some fall prey to the downfall of devastation.

If life isn't interesting, you're not trying hard enough.

Pick yourself back up when times get rough.

We only get one chance to live this life.

Too short to fill with pain and strife.

Find the beauty that exists all around us.

A river, a meadow, and even graffiti on a bus.

Just open your eyes and see things clear.

Make a change for the good and don't live in fear.

Even when the end is near.

Avoid the people that bring you down.

Rid yourself of the ones that attack your self-esteem
to steal your crown.

Being ridiculed and treated like a clown.

Talking to a human like they don't matter will make them shutdown.

Daily drinking to mask reality results in being facedown.

Judging a person for a single act and placing them
forever on lockdown.

Fighting to let anybody but your own live uptown.

Swimming in negativity will eventually make a person drown.

The way we're going society will experience a social meltdown.

Doesn't matter if you are black, white or brown.

Everyone should be a part of the rundown.

Furious at the world because leaders have made poor choices.

Making decisions for profit instead of listening to the masses of voices.

Consuming this world so the poor pay the price.

All along the lords living on high and not thinking twice.

Maintaining a ridiculous standard of living.

With a measly scrap to charity creates the illusion of giving.

More money to the blue collars will increase productivity and moral.

Maybe you don't need a billion horses in the corral.

There is enough for everyone to be satisfied.

How is "having it all" justified?

Emit love without judgement or hate.

If you fill your heart with love, then a full life is surely your fate.

I am a Caucasian man.
I am not saying this because I can.
Not the one that other sexes and races like to portray.
That is for some hooligans and the games they like to play.
I am a man that is about ethics.
Not just all about athletics.
I am the latter part of the word human.
Not the guy that calls out Noonan
Possessing a conscience and a soul.
Good deeds in the underlying goal.
So don't get a bad impression.
I won't judge you with some predetermined expression.
We are all the same.
Live righteous so you're not the one to blame.

Disappointed in the human race.

Endless greed for power and riches so you can own anyone and any place.

Rodney King asked, "Can't we all just get along?".

If we as a people lived by that, humanity would be strong.

This world has enough space and resources for everyone if we just share.

But it seems the wealthy want to horde things, offering scraps and charity pretending to care.

Everyone is unique and deserves respect as the person they are.

So, stop instantly labeling and judging one another at work, online, or walking down the street to your car.

We are all in this together.

Wouldn't harmony and sincerity make business more efficient and life in the community better?

Only the devil profits from hatred and torment.

Moguls caring more about profit margins above a targeted percent.

It's the people who truly drive the company where the treatment and compensation should be decent.

No one is better than anyone else.

It doesn't matter how prestigiously labeled a person is, we are all the same including yourself.

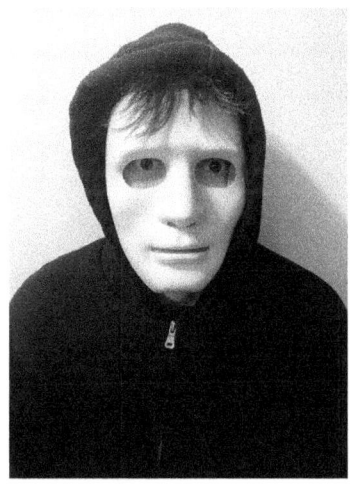

You're never wrong to do the right thing.
Making your conscience sing.
What you feel in your heart to be true.
Even if it has negative reactions upon you.
Don't worry what people may say.
Enabling you to grow wiser and help others one day.
Be confident in your decision and don't let your opinion fade.
Your soul feeling content with the choice that you've made.

People without power have no voice.

Whether individuals hear their words is not their choice.

It's not that they don't have something to say.

Eyes only focused on the color they see and the bills they can't pay.

Authorities on a power trip with a prejudiced agenda.

Just choosing to shut their eyes and enjoy their coffee with Splenda.

We are in a crisis.

Not from a foreign attack from Al Qaeda or Isis.

The world is crying out for help through the voices of scientists.

Powerful leaders holding environmental conferences wearing the crown of the protagonist.

Profits first, people second, and the world suffers from the misuse.

Our planet can't take much more of this abuse.

If the rich and powerful so-called leaders don't hear the powerless and their overwhelming voice.

Whether we still have the luxuries of food, water, and a sustainable planet is their choice.

Corporate Kangaroos climbing over each other to get up the ladder.

With the mentality that consumers and blue collars do not matter.

Money and the bottom line lead the way.

Having security that they don't have to worry
about the bills they have to pay.

Stomping on families and innocent lives.

Just hiring a person you know instead of going
through hundreds of applications

and replies.

All the while making money with no regard for the environment.

Just to get to a quicker retirement.

The coldness of their actions.

Doesn't soothe the stress of hard workers or appease their
satisfactions.

Be mindful of marketing ads and smooth hypnotic persuasions.

Think for yourself and make your own independent interpretations.

Avoid being trapped into following those corporate
kangaroos up the creaky

ladder.

It will only lead to an icy soul and personal lives shattered.

Why can't you look me in the eye?
The world has turned cold is the reason why.
Passing by one another on the street.
Am I not to your standards to greet?
My appearance looks clean and neat.
So why can't you look me in the eye?
It hurts me, I can't lie.
Is it the lack of respect or that I'm not good enough?
Or is it the color of my skin or that I look tough?
Maybe because of all the violence, and no one trusts another.
Or someone you just won't talk to like an ex-lover.
Why can't you look me in the eye?
It's not hard and could be enlightening if you try.

You cannot tell me to keep quiet.

Just because another's words started a riot.

Trying to help the boys and cheer on the team.

All while keeping the banter positive and clean.

Frustrating watching the politics unfold.

With the powerless having to do what they're told.

Kids putting in the extra work outside of practice sessions.

And not getting a fair shot sends these players into depressions.

The horrible antics performed by the coaches and administrators.

Gives these kids lifelong mental issues like they
are enslaved by a dictator.

The lasting effect of their actions and words could be
devastating to these kids.

Who knows what they would have accomplished or did.

With high school sports in full swing.

Scaring and bullying kids might not be the energy you want to bring.

Guidance

Advice to the people.

Are you living ethically?

Or doesn't it matter because you worship a steeple?

Are you proud of what you have done?

Do you have a plan to meet your goals for the future?

Doesn't matter if you've won.

If your opponent goes home with a suture.

We should raise the righteous person and praise them for sharing.

Cast down the hate for your fellow man letting yourself be open to kindness and caring.

Seeing a human with no attached labels.

Instead of bad mouthing and telling fables.

Treat people with respect and how you would like to be treated.

Before all the humanity in this world is depleted.

Consumer lives matter.

A shout out to big business.

We are the ones putting bread in your pocket.

Ours are the lives you shatter.

The people who struggle and save.

Only for you to put a price raise on the docket.

We are important too.

Not just stock prices and overhead.

Stop raping the innocent.

Give us the respect and the wage we are due.

Start embracing consumers as an equal.

Lending a hand to make lives better.

Just takes some compassion.

So, this empire doesn't end up a sequel.

This is a resurrection.

You can't hide behind the sins of your reflection.

We all are longing for acceptance and that sense of connection.

Love as been the righteous path since our conception.

You must be willing to consider evidence contrary to all your beliefs.

Understanding the admission of wrongdoing could cause you grief.

Being intelligent doesn't mean you know it all.

It's the ability to challenge what you know to be the law.

The clarity of the influx of knowledge propels one to question
personal imperfections.

The lack of presence and breathing will lead to anxiety and
hypertension.

This newfound maturity will spark a self-driven intervention.

The answers await within you based off your perception.

Poems for humanity.
Because we have turned this world into calamity.
The amount of corruption at the expense of humans is pure insanity.
Even kind words for a president are nothing less than a profanity.
Political parties need to compromise their duality.
The disregard for life is a harsh reality.
Selflessness is replaced whole heartly by vanity.
The few rule the many despite government's riches and brutality.
Not repairing the earth will end in our mortality.
When it's too late we will understand the gravity.

about the author

Brian Geerdts

Humble beginnings politely describes his upbringing in Southeast Wisconsin.

Creative soul that searched for his place in the world that would allow him to help better society.

Through hard work, perseverance, and dedication; Brian has made a career as a freelancer working nationally and internationally in the sports broadcasting industry.

Brian believes that whatever endeavor a person wants to focus on, make sure you put your heart and soul into being the best at it as you can possibly be. Even striving to go beyond your given abilities. Reach for perfection.

His writing was compelled from the love and pain experienced in this world. Seen through his eyes, felt in his heart, and expressed with his mind. Typed with his fingers so you, the reader can hear his message of humanity.

www.ingramcontent.com/pod-product-compliance
Lightning Source LLC
Chambersburg PA
CBHW051221120626
46547CB00013B/1452